Money Management for Teenage Girls

A Comprehensive Guide to Budgeting, Saving, and Personal Finance for a Bright Future

Table of Contents

Introduction

As you enter your teenage years, you start dealing with all sorts of new things, including money. As exciting as it is, a thorough understanding of managing your money lays the groundwork for a financially secure future. Basically speaking, you don't want to go broke. Money can sometimes feel intimidating and confusing to some people, but it doesn't have to be that way. This book is here to break it down for you, step by step, and give you the skills and knowledge you need to make the smartest financial choices and chart a course to a financially stable tomorrow.

Why is money management so important, you might ask? Well, say you're hanging out with your friends, and suddenly, they all decide to go to that awesome concert you've been dying to attend. But, uh-oh . . . you don't have enough cash to join the fun. Talk about a bummer. But fear not, because, with the right money management skills, you'll be free to say "count me in" to those amazing experiences without worrying about your bank account.

As you read this book, you'll learn about budgeting, saving, and setting goals. You'll understand how to make your money work for you, maybe through earning income, starting a side hustle, or investing. This book will also demystify the ins and outs of credit scores and other financial mumbo-jumbo that you're bound to run into as you grow older. But it isn't just about numbers and calculations. This book is about you and your journey towards financial independence. The goal is to help you develop a healthy, positive mindset around money. This book ensures you understand the concepts and how they relate to your life experiences.

Learning about money shouldn't be boring or intimidating; it should be fun and easy. So, come aboard the money train to financial independence.

Your life is about to change.

Chapter One: Money 101

Imagine for a second that you're in a big game of make-believe, and in this game, everyone has their own special skills or things they can do. Some people are really good at growing food, others are excellent at making clothes, and some are super talented at fixing things. Now, all of you need food, clothes, and other things to live comfortably, right? But what if the person who grows the best fruits doesn't really need any clothes, and the person who makes stylish clothes isn't hungry?

That's where money comes in.

Money is a widely accepted currency that people use every day to obtain things they need, like clothes, food, or concert tickets. It's special in that it makes trading and buying stuff easier. Instead of exchanging items directly, for example, a cup of water for a slice of bread, you can use money to represent the value of the things you want or the things you can offer.

Before the concept of money was invented, people used to trade products with each other.

This form of exchange has been around for a while now. Back in ancient times, people traded goods directly. Maybe if you had extra wheat and needed some pottery, you would have to find someone who had pottery and wanted wheat. It seems pretty straightforward, but it can get very complicated very quickly. So, people came up with an idea: they started using objects like seashells or shiny rocks as a form of currency. This made trading much simpler because everyone agreed that those objects had value, so you could bring, say, three seashells and get some wheat. Eventually, people moved on to using metal coins and, later on, paper money and coins made of different materials.

But the thing is, money doesn't have value just because it's made of metal or paper. Its value comes from the trust and agreement that society has. Society believes that money can be exchanged for goods and services, so it is accepted to trade and buy things. Money makes getting the things you want easier because you can use it to buy from anyone, not just the person who wants what you have. It's a common language that everyone understands. When you see a price tag on something, it tells you how much money you need to give to get that item. This system allows you to compare prices and make clever choices when you buy things. Money tells you how valuable things are, whether getting a pizza or a brand-new skateboard. It helps you decide what to buy and how much to spend. Plus, it saves you from the hassle of bartering, which is when you swap things directly with someone else.

Types of Money

- **Cash:** First, there is good old cash – those paper bills and shiny coins you might have in your purse or piggy bank. Cash is the most basic form of money. It is used to buy things directly. You can pay for a snack at the school cafeteria or get a cool T-shirt at the mall. It's also handy because you can physically hold it and use it anytime, anywhere.

- **Digital Money:** Next up is something called "digital money." This is money that exists in electronic form. It is super convenient because, with it, you don't need to carry cash around. With digital money, you can buy all sorts of things online without leaving your couch. Need some new shoes? Just go to the online store, add them to your cart, and pay with your card or through a payment app. Digital money is also great for paying bills. With a few taps, you can set up automatic payments through your bank or use payment apps to settle your bills. Some would say it's the best thing about the 21st century.

- **Virtual Money:** Virtual money is the cooler, more futuristic sibling of digital money. It exists solely in the digital realm and isn't tied to any physical form. You might have heard about cryptocurrencies like Bitcoin or Ethereum. These are some of the most well-known types of virtual money out there. They're digital tokens that live on the internet and have their own unique value. People use virtual money for all sorts of online transactions, but some see it as more than just a means of buying stuff. They view it as an investment opportunity. People invest in stocks or real estate just as you might invest in cryptocurrencies. They believe that the value of virtual money will grow over time, and they hope to make some serious profit. It's a whole new frontier in finance. It's exciting but also a bit of a wild ride.

When it comes to picking the type of money to use, it's your decision to choose what you feel comfortable using.
https://pixabay.com/photos/money-card-pocket-concept-idea-256281/

When it comes to picking the type of money to use, it's your decision to choose what you feel comfortable using. Some people prefer cash because it's tangible and feels real. Others love using their debit or credit cards because it's convenient, and they don't have to carry around a bunch of coins or bills. Simply choose what works best in different situations. If you're shopping online, digital money is the way to go. And if you're out with friends and need to split the bill, apps like Venmo can make it a breeze. No matter what type of money you use, you need to be responsible about it. Keep track of your spending, and make sure you're not spending more than you have. Always think twice before making a big purchase. Money is a tool, and like every other tool, proper handling is vital.

Rookie Financial Terms You Should Know

- **Income:** Income is the money you earn or receive – the flow of money coming into your pocket. It is the allowance you get from your parents, the money you make from a part-time job, or even the cash you receive as a birthday gift. Basically, it's any money that comes your way.

- **Expenses:** On the flip side, you have expenses. You spend your money on these things, like food, going out with friends, or paying your phone bill. Whenever money leaves your pocket, it's considered an expense.

- **Budget:** A budget is a plan for your money. It helps you track how to spend and save your hard-earned cash so you can still have fun while being responsible.

- **Savings:** Savings are the money you set aside for the future. You might save up for something special, like a new laptop or a dream vacation. Savings help you prepare for unexpected expenses and achieve your long-term goals.

Why is having an income so important? An income gives you the power to make choices and take care of yourself. It allows you to buy the things you need and want. It also gives you independence and the ability to save for your future. If you didn't have any money coming in, you wouldn't be able to buy the things you really want or save up for anything. You would have to rely entirely on whoever provides the cash. In itself, that is not a bad thing, especially at a young age, but the sooner you start earning an income and learning how to manage it, the better prepared you'll be for when you're much older. An income gives you the freedom to make your own decisions and be in control of your financial life. It also teaches you essential life skills, like budgeting and managing your money wisely. You'll understand the value of hard work and responsibility and discover even more ways to make your income work for you.

Why Is Financial Literacy Important?

1. **Take Charge of Your Money:** You're in control when you're financially literate. You have the power to make decisions you wouldn't be able to make if you didn't have the funds. You can decide to save for something special or plan for your future.

2. **Avoid Money Traps:** Financial literacy helps you avoid common mistakes that can lead to debt and financial trouble. You'll learn how to manage your money properly, understand interest rates, and make responsible choices regarding borrowing.

3. **Plan for Your Dreams:** Want to travel the world, start your own business, or buy a home someday? Financial literacy helps you turn those dreams into reality. You'll learn how to set goals, make a plan, and take steps toward achieving them.

4. **Grow Your Wealth:** Being financially literate means understanding how to make your money work for you. You'll learn about investing, retirement saving, compound interest, and its power. Building wealth becomes an exciting possibility.

5. **Understand the Money Maze:** Financial literacy helps you make sense of all those confusing financial terms and systems. You'll understand how banks work, how credit cards and insurance function, and even how taxes play a role in your financial life.

6. **Shop Smart:** Knowing how to manage your money means you're a savvy consumer. You'll be able to spot good deals, avoid scams, and make better purchase decisions.

7. **Stress Less:** Money can be a big source of stress, but you'll feel more confident and in control if you know what you're doing. You'll have everything you need to manage your money, handle unexpected expenses, and build a safety net. Financial peace of mind is a real thing.

8. **Pass It On:** When financially literate, you can share your knowledge with your friends, family, and future generations. It's a gift that keeps on giving.

9. **Be a Stable Force:** Financially literate people contribute to a stable economy. By making sound financial choices, managing debt responsibly, and being a smart shopper, you're doing your part to create a stronger economic future for everyone.

10. **Live Your Best Life:** At the end of the day, financial literacy is about living your best life. It's about having the freedom and confidence to chase your dreams, enjoy the things that matter to you, and have peace of mind knowing that your financial house is in order.

This book is here to give you a little boost of motivation when it comes to managing your money. It will take some time and effort, and you might stumble along the way, but this skill is worth every trial and error because it will benefit you for the rest of your amazing life. It takes practice; sure, you might make a few mistakes while you're at it, but every time you try, you'll get better and better. These skills will stick with you throughout your life, and with each lesson learned, you'll become more confident and savvy with your finances.

Chapter Two: Creating a Budget

A budget is a detailed outline of your income and your expenses. It's a plan that helps you track how much money you have coming in and how much you're spending. This plan is incredibly useful for several reasons, including:

- **It Helps You Track Your Spending:** You can see exactly where your money goes with a budget. It keeps tabs on your expenses so you don't end up wondering where all your money went. You'll know exactly how much you're spending.

- **It Helps You Save Money:** Budgets are great for saving up for things you want or need. Say you want to buy a new video game or save up for a summer trip with your friends. A budget can help you set aside monthly money specifically for those goals.

- **It Prevents Overspending:** Have you ever spent all your money and wished you had saved even a little bit? A budget can help you avoid that. By setting spending limits for different categories, like eating out or shopping, you'll be more aware of how much you can afford to spend at any given time.

Types of Budgets

- **Personal Budget:** This is a money plan for yourself. It helps you track all the money you earn – your allowance or money from doing chores, for example – and figure out how you want to spend it.

BUDGET FOR WEEK(S) OF _____

INCOME

Income Source	Planned Amount	Actual Earned
Totals:		

EXPENSES

Expense	Planned Amount	Actual Spent	Leak or Leftover
Totals:			

SAVINGS

Planned Savings:

Leftover Money Not Spent:

Actual Money Put Into Savings:

Money to Carry Over to Next Budget Cycle:

- **Household Budget:** This is a money plan for the whole family. With this budget, you can work out how much money the family has coming in - from jobs or other sources and decide how to spend it wisely. A household budget includes rent, electricity, groceries, and maybe planning for a family vacation or birthday.

- **Business Budget:** This is a financial plan for a company or business. Businesses must know how much money they expect to make and how they'll spend it. This budget helps them with a few things, including buying supplies, paying employees, and making sure they turn a profit.

How to Create a Budget

Budgeting might sound like a lot, but it is an easy and absolutely necessary skill that can take you places. Whether you're saving up for something special or simply want to keep tabs on your money, here's a step-by-step guide to creating an achievable budget that will serve you well:

1. Determine Your Financial Goals

What do you want to achieve with your money? Are you saving for something specific or just building up an emergency fund? Knowing what you want will help you stay motivated and focused.

2. Write Down Your Income

Make a list of all the money you receive regularly. This can include allowances, money from part-time jobs, or any other source of income. Be sure to include the amounts and how often you receive them, like weekly or monthly.

3. List Your Expenses

Write down all the things you spend money on regularly. This can include clothing, Netflix, transportation, and any other expenses you have. Be honest and include everything to clearly understand where your money is going.

4. Differentiate between Needs and Wants

Separate your expenses into two categories: needs and wants. Needs like food, housing, and school supplies are fundamental and non-negotiable. Wants are things that you would like to have but aren't necessary. This separation will help you prioritize your spending.

5. Set Spending Limits

Now that you know your income and expenses, it's time to set limits for each category. Put a certain amount of money into each expense category based on how much you have and your priorities. Leave a little room for savings.

6. Track Your Spending

Keep track of your expenses as you spend money. Write down what you spend and in which category. This will help you see if you're staying within your budget and make adjustments if necessary.

7. Review and Adjust Regularly

Find time to review your budget monthly and see how well you're sticking to it. Adjust your spending limits if necessary. It's okay to make changes as you learn more about your spending habits.

Budgeting Methods

There are different budgeting methods to choose from when creating your budget. Here are a few popular ones:

- **The "50-30-20" Budget:** This type of budget suggests dividing your income into three categories. You spend 50% on *essentials* (must-haves) like rent and groceries, 30% on things you want but don't necessarily need, like movies or new clothes, and

20% on savings or debt. It's a balanced approach to managing your money.

- **The "Envelope" Budget:** This budgeting method involves using physical envelopes to divide specific amounts of money for different expenses. For example, you might have an envelope for groceries, one for entertainment, and one for savings. Once an envelope is empty, you know you've reached your limit for that category.

- **The "Zero-Based" Budget:** This approach involves using every dollar of your income for a specific purpose. It means giving each dollar a job, like bills, savings, or even treating yourself. The goal is to ensure your income minus expenses equals zero, so you're being intentional with every dollar you earn.

Tips on How to Stick to Your Budget

Sticking to a budget and staying within your limits can be a bit of a challenge, but with some useful tips, it'll be as easy as brushing your teeth. Here's what you need to know:

- **Track Your Expenses:** Keep a record of everything you spend. It could be as simple as jotting down your purchases in a notebook or using a budgeting app on your phone. By knowing where your money is going, you can make better decisions and avoid overspending.

- **Prioritize Your Spending:** Remember, there's a difference between needs and wants. Before making a purchase, ask yourself if it's something you truly need or if it's more of a want. If it's a want, does it align with your financial goals or budget? The answer to that question will help you focus your money on what matters most to you.

- **Plan Your Meals:** Eating out can quickly drain your wallet. Instead, plan your meals and eat at home as much as you can. Not only is it usually healthier, but it's also a great way to save money.

- **Avoid Impulse Buying:** It's easy to get tempted by something shiny or trendy, but before making an impulse purchase, give yourself some time to think it over. Ask yourself if it's something you truly need or just a spur-of-the-moment desire. Waiting a day or two can help you make a more thoughtful decision.

- **Find Affordable:** Alternatives: When it comes to shopping, look for sales, discounts, and thrift stores. You'll be surprised at the amazing deals you can find. Also, consider borrowing or swapping items with friends instead of buying them brand new. It's a fun way to save money while still enjoying new things.

- **Build a Supportive Network:** Share your budgeting goals with your friends and family. Having a support network can keep you motivated and accountable. You can even make it a fun challenge by organizing budget-friendly activities together, like movie nights at home or hosting a yard sale.

- **Celebrate Small Wins:** Budgeting is a journey, and your progress deserves to be acknowledged. Treat yourself to a small reward when you meet your savings goals or stick to your monthly budget. It can be anything, as long as it doesn't break the bank.

What Is an Emergency Fund?

An emergency fund is a financial safety net that protects you from unexpected expenses without throwing your budget off track. You never know when something random might happen. It could be a health issue, a broken phone, or even a family crisis. These things can cost money, and having an emergency fund helps you be prepared. You can start building your emergency fund by setting aside a little bit of money from your allowance or any money you receive as gifts. Over time, it adds up and becomes your safety cushion. The goal is to have enough money in your emergency fund to cover a few months' worth of expenses, just in case.

Here's how to build your own emergency fund:

- **Start Small and Be Consistent:** Building an emergency fund doesn't happen overnight, so don't worry if you can't save a huge amount immediately. Start small by setting aside a portion of your monthly income, even if it's just a few dollars. The key is to be consistent and make saving a habit.

- **Set a Savings Goal:** Decide on a specific amount you want to save for your emergency fund. Aiming for at least three to six months' worth of living expenses is generally recommended. This way, you'll have enough money to cover necessary future expenses that fall outside your budget.

- **Cut Back on Unnecessary Expenses:** Look at your budget and identify areas where you can cut back on unnecessary expenses. You'll make faster progress by redirecting that money to your emergency fund.

- **Save Extra Income:** Whenever you receive unexpected money, like birthday gifts, bonuses, or even money from odd jobs, consider putting a portion (or all of it!) into your emergency fund. It's a great way to boost your savings without affecting your regular budget.

- **Make Adjustments as You Go:** As you save and your financial situation changes, adjusting your savings goals or the amount you contribute to your emergency fund is okay. Your priorities may shift. Just make sure you're consistently putting money aside for those unexpected situations.

- **Keep Your Emergency Fund Separate:** To avoid dipping into your emergency fund for non-emergency expenses, keep it in a separate place. This way, you'll be less tempted to use the money for something else and know it's there when you truly need it.

With a budget, you become the boss of your money. You'll have a clear plan for every dollar and make the best choices about spending it. No more impulse buying or regretting those random purchases. Instead, you'll be able to prioritize your spending based on what's truly important to you and avoid that sinking feeling of regret when you realize you have no clue where all your money went.

Chapter Three: Spending Wisely and Saving

Wise Spending

Wise spending means being intentional and thoughtful about where your money goes.
https://www.pexels.com/photo/person-putting-coin-in-a-piggy-bank-1602726/

When you've worked hard for your money, it's natural to want to make the most of it, and you can only do that if you spend it wisely. Wise spending means being intentional and thoughtful about where your money goes. It doesn't mean depriving yourself of everything you enjoy. It means finding a balance between your needs and wants. The keywords here are moderation and prioritization. To be a wise spender, you should be able to:

- **Differentiate between Needs and Wants:** Distinguish between essential items or services necessary for your survival (needs) and those that are nice to have but not essential (wants). More on this later.

- **Research and Compare Prices:** Doing your homework and comparing prices is another key aspect. Everyone loves a good deal, right? Then, take the time to research and shop around before making a purchase. Look for discounts, coupons, or even alternative items that offer similar quality but at a lower cost.

- **Consider Long-Term Value:** Instead of getting caught up in the excitement of the moment, take a step back and consider the long-term value of what you're buying. Sure, that purchase might give you an instant thrill, but will it still be useful and relevant a year from now? Ask yourself, "Will this purchase bring lasting benefits to my life, or will it lose its shine sooner than I expect?"

- **Choose Quality Over Quantity:** When it comes to quality, it's not always about going for the cheapest option. Sometimes, investing more upfront can save you money in the long run. Consider the durability and lifespan of what you're buying. Opting for higher-quality items might mean spending a bit more initially, but they often last longer and require fewer replacements.

- **Prioritize Experiences Over Material Possessions:** Don't get caught up in the race for material possessions. Instead, lean toward experiences that create lasting happiness. When you look back on your life, it will be the memories of incredible adventures, trying new things, and sharing beautiful moments that stay with you. Think about the laughter, the stories, and the connections you make during these experiences. They become a part of who you are, unlike material wants that may lose their sparkle over time. Nobody is saying you have to completely give up on material things. Rather, you need to find a balance and recognize the true value of experiences in your life.

Essential Needs and Non-Essential Wants

When you go grocery shopping with a limited budget, you must be clear on what you need versus what you just want. Essential needs are the things that are necessary for you to survive and live a healthy life. These include food, water, clothing, shelter, and basic healthcare. These are the must-haves that are required for your well-being and safety. On the other hand, non-essential wants are things that are nice to have, but you can live without them. These are the extras, like a cute but expensive new top, eating out at restaurants, or going to the movies. They add a little flair to the loop of daily existence, but they're not essential for survival.

Your needs must be a priority in your budget. This way, you ensure you have enough money to cover the essential things first. By taking care of your needs, you are:

1. **Paying Attention to Your Financial Security:** Taking care of your essential needs first means you have a roof over your head, food on your table, and the necessary resources to stay healthy. It provides a sense of security and stability in your life. While your parents/guardians are providing for your needs now, it won't be long before you'll be taking care of yourself!

2. **Responsibly Managing Money:** By focusing on your needs in your budget, you're learning how to be smart with your money. You are developing good financial habits and ensuring that you have the means to cover your necessary expenses.

3. **Making Space for Your Wants:** Prioritizing your needs does not mean completely giving up what you enjoy. It's more about establishing a middle ground. Once your needs are taken care of, you can funnel a portion of your budget into your wants, allowing you to enjoy the extras without compromising your financial security.

4. **Becoming a Better Decision-Maker:** Making smart financial decisions is easier when you know what really matters in your budget. By figuring out what expenses are essential, you'll make better choices with your money, and it becomes easier to think about the pros and cons of spending on non-essential things.

5. **Financially Disciplined:** When you prioritize your needs, you become more disciplined and controlled in your spending habits. You learn the difference between what you really need and what is an impulse. This skill makes it easier to resist buying things on a whim and instead make thoughtful spending decisions.

6. **Setting a Positive Example:** When you have a budget and stick to it, you become a role model for your family and friends. You inspire and motivate them to do the same by showing them how to handle money responsibly.

Tips and Tricks for Smart Spending Habits

These tips will help you shop smart, avoid impulse buying, and make cost-effective decisions when spending your money.

1. **Make a Shopping List:** Before you head out to buy anything, make a list of what you really need. This way, you'll be less likely to get distracted by other things that catch your eye. Stick to your list, and you'll avoid buying unnecessary stuff.

2. **Do Your Research:** When you're eyeing something you want to buy, research it first. Look for reviews, compare prices from different stores, and see if any discounts or deals are available. This way, you can make sure you're getting the best value for your money.

3. **Avoid Impulse Buying:** Those tempting impulse buys can be hard to resist. One trick is to give yourself some time before making a purchase. When you see something you want, wait a day or two. If you still really want it after that time, then go ahead and buy it. But usually, you'll find that the impulse fades, and you'll save yourself some money.

4. **Cook at Home:** Eating out can feel like the best thing ever - but the costs can also add up quickly. Instead of always eating out, try eating at - or cooking at - home more often. It is usually cheaper and a great way to learn new skills, bond with your family or friends, and experiment with delicious recipes. Plus, you get to control the ingredients and make healthier choices.

5. **Set a Spending Limit:** It's easy to get carried away when shopping or browsing online. To avoid overspending, set a spending limit for yourself. Decide how much you're willing to spend on a particular shopping trip or item and stick to it. This way, you'll stay within your budget and avoid regrets later.

6. **Consider Secondhand Options:** Don't forget about secondhand options when shopping for clothes or other items. Thrift stores, online marketplaces, and clothing swaps can offer great deals and exciting finds. Not only will you save money, but you'll also be reducing waste and giving pre-loved items a new home.

7. **Save for Big-Ticket Items:** If there's something expensive you really want, like a new phone or a gaming console, consider saving up for it instead of buying it on impulse.

Set aside a portion of your allowance or earnings regularly until you reach your goal. It might take some time, but it will feel even more rewarding when you finally get what you've been saving for.

Smart Saving

Saving money is not only beneficial but also empowering. Savings provide a safety net for unexpected situations or emergencies. Your savings allow you to handle these situations without feeling overwhelmed or resorting to debt. Saving also helps you reach certain financial milestones. For instance, you may dream of attending college one day or buying something nice for yourself. Saving money is the key to making those dreams a reality.

Practical Strategies to Help You Save Money

- **Pay Yourself First:** When you receive money, whether from an allowance, a part-time job, or a gift, make it a habit to set aside a little for savings before spending on anything else. Treat it as a priority. This strategy will ensure you're consistently saving and building your financial foundation.

- **Track Your Expenses:** Keep track of what you spend your money on. It could be as simple as using a notebook or a budgeting app on your phone. By tracking your expenses, you become more aware of where your money is going and can identify areas where you can cut back or make adjustments to save more.

- **Cut Unnecessary Expenses:** Check your spending habits and note any costs that aren't necessary. It could be frequent eating out or impulse purchases. Do any of these expenses align with your priorities and goals? If not, find ways to cut back or eliminate them altogether. For example, you could cook more meals at home or borrow books from the library instead of buying them.

- **Set Savings Goals:** A specific savings goal gives you something to work towards and motivates you to save. It could be saving a certain amount of money by a particular date or for a specific item or experience. Break your goals down into smaller milestones and celebrate each achievement as you make it. This will keep you inspired and excited about your progress.

- **Find Creative Ways to Save:** Look for opportunities to save money in your daily life. For instance, you could save loose change in a jar, participate in money-saving challenges, or find free or low-cost alternatives for entertainment and activities. Get creative and think outside the box.

Saving money is a skill that will never let you down, especially as you grow older. When you make saving a habit, you become more independent and confident in managing your own money. And as you continue to save, you'll start to see amazing results. One of the first things you'll notice is the peace of mind it brings. You'll feel secure knowing you have a contingency plan in case of unexpected expenses or emergencies. Say goodbye to those sleepless nights worrying about money and hello to a kind of peace that only money can bring.

Saving money also gives you a sense of pride and fulfillment. You can save up for an epic trip, fund your education, or start your own business. Every single thing you achieve boosts your confidence and reminds you that you have what it takes to make things happen. Internalize the idea of saving money and watch how it transforms your life. It's not just about the numbers in your bank account; it's the freedom, security, and endless possibilities that come with it. Start today and thank yourself later.

Chapter Four: Investing Made Simple

You want to take enough risk to have the potential for higher returns but not so much risk that you're uncomfortable or threaten your financial future.

https://pixabay.com/photos/money-coin-investment-business-2724241/

The whole idea behind investing revolves around finding the right balance between risk and return. You want to take enough risk to have the potential for higher returns but not so much risk that you're uncomfortable or threaten your financial future. As an investor, you'll be playing a long-term game. It's not a get-rich-quick scheme, so patience and discipline are the keywords here. To become a good investor, there are some principles you must follow. Understanding these principles will help you make smarter investment decisions. The principles of investing are:

- **Risk:** When you invest, there's always a chance that you might not get all the money you put back in. Think of it like a game. In some games, you must take chances, and it's the same with investing. Different investments have different levels of risk. For example, investing in stocks can be riskier than putting money in a savings account. You should know how comfortable you are with taking risks before choosing where to invest.

- **Return:** Return is what you hope to earn from your investments. It's the profit or the extra money you make on top of what you initially invested. The amount you can earn depends on the type of investment you choose. Usually, investments that have higher risk also have the potential for higher returns. But remember, higher returns also mean a higher chance of losing money.

- **Time Value of Money:** This might sound confusing, but it's pretty simple. It means that the money you have now is worth more than the money you'll get in the future. Why? Because when you have money now, you can do things with it, like invest and make more money over time. But if you don't have the money now or have to wait to get it later, you miss out on the chance to grow it. So, starting to invest early is a great idea. The more time you give your investments to grow, the more money you can potentially make.

What Can a Teenager Invest in?

As a teenager, there are different things you can invest in. While some options might have age restrictions or require help from adults, there are still ways for you to get started. Here are some common types of investments, along with what you can and cannot invest in yet:

- **Stocks:** Stocks are a way to become a part-owner of a company. It means you have a little piece of the company for yourself. *But since you're not an adult yet, you'll need the help of an adult to invest in stocks.* They will set up a custodial account, which lets them manage the stocks on your behalf until you're old enough to take over. When choosing which stocks to invest in, you might be familiar with companies like Apple or Facebook because they're famous and many people use their products. These are popular choices as investments. Another option is an ETF, which stands for Exchange Traded Fund. It's a basket of stocks that are grouped together. Investing in an ETF allows you to spread out your investment across many different companies, which can be a good way to reduce risk.

- **Bonds:** Bonds are easily defined as the loans you give to companies or governments. It's a way for them to borrow money from you. *As with stocks, you'll need an adult to help you invest in bonds through a custodial account.* You can invest in US Treasury bonds, which are loans to the government, or you can choose to invest in bonds from companies. When you invest in bonds, you're basically lending them money. In return, they promise to repay you the money you loaned plus a little extra over a certain period. Bonds are considered a more stable and predictable investment compared to stocks. They can be a good choice if you want to earn extra money on your savings but don't want as much risk as you might have with stocks.

- **Mutual Funds:** Mutual funds are a collection of different investments bundled together. Think of a team of investors working to help you grow your money. Some mutual funds have rules about how much money you need to invest, making it hard for a teenager. *Luckily, there are mutual funds specifically designed for young investors like you.* These funds allow you to invest with smaller amounts of money, which makes it more accessible for you to get started. One type of mutual fund popular with young investors is a target-date fund. This fund automatically adjusts your investments as you get closer to retirement age. So, as you grow older, the fund will gradually shift your investments to be more conservative, which means they aim to protect your money rather than taking big risks. Target-date funds are great because they do the work of managing your investments for you. You don't have to worry too much about choosing individual stocks or bonds. Instead, you can rely on the fund professionals to make those decisions based on your target retirement date.

- **Real Estate:** Investing in real estate involves buying properties to make money. *As a teenager, it's not feasible, but there's an alternative called a REIT.* A REIT, which stands for Real Estate Investment Trust, is a company that owns different types of properties, such as shopping malls, office buildings, or apartments. When you invest in a REIT, you're essentially buying company shares. This allows you to be involved in the real estate market without buying a property on your own. Investing in REITs can be done with the help of an adult who can guide you through the process. It's a way to indirectly invest in real estate and benefit from the income generated by the properties owned by the REIT. As a shareholder, you will receive your share of the rental income collected from the properties.

- **Alternative Investments:** These are different from the usual ones, like stocks and bonds. Examples include gold, oil, or even cryptocurrency like Bitcoin. However, alternative investments can be riskier and need more research, so it's better to be careful and get advice from adults or professionals before considering them.

Investment Strategies

Every investment strategy has its own unique approach, and there's no one-size-fits-all strategy. So, it's good to think about your financial goals, risk tolerance, and time frame when choosing a plan. Some people even combine different strategies based on their preferences and needs. Understanding these strategies will help you decide how best to grow your money. Here are a few:

- **Long-Term Investing:** Think of long-term investing as a marathon, not a sprint. This strategy involves holding onto your investments for longer, like years or even decades. Treat it like a garden where you plant seeds and care for them, hoping they will grow into beautiful trees. Long-term investing is perfect for saving up for big goals like a college education.

- **Value Investing:** Value investing is similar to being a smart shopper who knows how to spot a great deal. With this strategy, you search for stocks or investments you believe are overlooked or on sale – something everyone will want later; they just don't know it yet. Investing in undervalued assets and holding onto them can potentially earn a profit when their value increases.

- **Growth Investing:** Growth investing is about embracing the future and supporting companies with great potential. It's being an early supporter of a rising star. With this strategy, you look for companies or investments expected to experience rapid growth. Investing in an exciting new app or a sustainable fashion brand that you think will become a huge success is a good example. When you take a chance on growth-oriented ventures, you can benefit from their future success and see your investments grow with them.

Diversifying Investment Portfolios

Diversification is an important concept that can help you manage risks and potentially increase your returns. Imagine you're planning a party, and you want to make sure everyone has a good time. You wouldn't serve only one type of food or play just one type of music, would you? Of course not. You understand that people have different tastes and preferences. Well, the same idea applies to investing.

Creating a diversified investment portfolio is like throwing a party with lots of things to enjoy. Instead of putting all your money into just one investment, you spread it across different investments. You might invest in stocks, bonds, real estate, or other assets. By doing this, if one investment doesn't do well, you have others that might perform better and help balance things out. Diversification helps reduce the risk of losing all your money if one investment doesn't pan out. It's a way to protect yourself and potentially increase your chances of making money in the long run. If you'd like to diversify your investments, try these:

- **Mix Different Types of Investments:** You want to mix different investments in your portfolio, for example, stocks, bonds, and maybe even real estate investment trusts (REITs). This way, if one type of investment doesn't do well, the others might still be doing fine.

- **Invest in Different Industries or Sectors:** You want to invest in companies from various industries, like technology, healthcare, or consumer goods. Doing this means you're not relying on just one section to perform well. If one industry faces a hard time, others may still do well.

- **Consider Different Risk Levels:** Not all investments carry the same level of risk. Some investments, like stocks, can be more volatile, while others, like bonds, tend to be more stable. Aim to strike a balance that matches your risk tolerance and financial goals.

- **Regularly Review and Rebalance:** Just like you'd check if everyone at your party is having a good time, you should regularly review your portfolio. Over time, some investments may grow more than others, which can throw off your diversification. Rebalancing means adjusting your investments to bring them back in line with your original plan.

Defining Your Investment Goals

You are the CEO of your future. You have the power to make decisions that protect and improve your interests. When it comes to investing, it's the same thing. Your investment goals are the things you want to achieve with your money when you invest it. These goals should reflect your dreams for the future, your needs, and your values. Where to begin?

1. **Financial Needs:** Think about your financial needs. What are the things you want to achieve with your money? It could be anything from saving up for college, traveling the world, starting your own business, or supporting causes you care about. Knowing your financial needs will help you set specific investment goals to bring you closer to those dreams.

2. **Aspirations:** Next, your aspirations. What kind of life do you want for yourself? What are your long-term dreams and ambitions? Maybe you want to become a successful business mogul, chase a career in a specific field, or contribute positively to your community. Your investment goals should support your aspirations and help

you build the financial foundation to reach them.

3. **Personal Values:** It's advisable to put your money into companies or causes that match your beliefs. For instance, if you care about protecting the environment, you can invest in renewable energy or eco-friendly businesses. If you're passionate about social justice, you can look for investments that promote diversity and equality.

The Risks of Investing

Risk is an inherent part of the investment process, and every investor knows you can't have investments without some risk. So, what exactly is risk in the context of investing? Risk is the possibility of losing money or not getting the returns you hoped for when you invested. It is the uncertainty that comes with investing because there are things that can affect how your investments do, and you can't control them. For example, market conditions, how the global economy is doing, or even events that only affect specific companies. These factors all impact how your investments turn out, so before you invest, you should know what you're signing up for and the risks involved. There are:

1. **Market Risks:** This means that the value of your investments can go up and down because of factors like the economy, politics, or trends in specific industries. It's a roller coaster – it can be thrilling, but sometimes it can make your stomach drop. So, it's good to be prepared for the ups and downs in the investing world.

2. **Volatility Risks:** This is when investments have big price swings and can be a little unpredictable. Think of it like a mood swing – the fluctuations can be wild. Some investments are more volatile than others, so you should understand your risk tolerance and be ready for those price fluctuations.

3. **Liquidity Risks:** This means some investments might not be easy to sell quickly or at a good price. You can compare this to having a limited-edition item that's hard to sell

when you need the cash. For this risk, you need to think about how easily you can access your money if you need it quickly.

4. **Credit Risk:** This risk comes into play when dealing with bonds or loans. There is a possibility that the issuer might not be able to pay back what they owe. You don't want to lend money to people with a history of bad debt.

5. **Concentration Risk:** This happens when you put a chunk of your money into just one investment or specific area. If that investment doesn't do well, it can be bad news for your overall portfolio. Imagine putting all your eggs in one basket and dropping that basket. It's not a good idea, is it?

Tips to Manage Investment Risks

- **Spread Your Money:** Don't put all your money into one investment. Diversify by spreading it across different types of investments, like stocks, bonds, and real estate.

- **Know What You Want:** Set clear investment goals and consider how long you will wait. Short-term goals call for safer investments, while long-term goals can handle more risk.

- **Do Your Homework:** Research is your best friend. Dig deep into the companies you're considering investing in. Look at their track record, financial health, and what's happening in their industry. The more you know, the better the decisions you can make.

- **Stay in the Loop:** Keep an eye on what's happening in the market and the economy. Stay informed about any news or events that could affect your investments. Being aware helps you make adjustments early if the situation calls for it.

- **Get a Second Opinion:** Don't hesitate to get advice from the pros. A financial advisor will give you guidance tailored to your situation. They can teach you to navigate the investment world with more confidence.

- **Check-in Regularly:** Don't forget to review your investments periodically. Make sure they still match your goals and risk tolerance. Adjustments may be necessary based on changing circumstances.

- **Think Long-Term:** Again, investing is a marathon, not a sprint. Avoid knee-jerk reactions to short-term changes in the market. Focus on your long-term goals, and remember that patience pays off.

Chapter Five: Credit and Debt Management

Credit means borrowing money or getting a loan. It's when someone – a bank or a lender – gives you money with the understanding that you'll pay it back later. This is useful when you need extra money to buy something but don't have all the cash upfront. It allows you to make big purchases, like a car or a house, or handle unexpected expenses, like medical bills or home repairs.

When you use credit, you're essentially using someone else's money to pay for things, *but it's not free money.* You have to pay it back, usually with an extra amount added, which is called *interest.* To get credit, lenders will look at your creditworthiness. They want to know if you're a reliable borrower who will pay the money back on time. They check your credit history, which shows how you've handled credit in the past. If you've paid your bills on time and managed your debts responsibly, you'll have a good credit history, which makes it easier to get credit in the future. Good credit is essential because it can affect your ability to get loans, rent an apartment, or even get a job. A good credit score equals a good reputation for being responsible with money.

Credit means borrowing money or getting a loan.
https://www.pexels.com/photo/person-signing-loan-agreement-for-purchase-of-apartment-5849563/

There are different forms of credit: credit cards and loans. A credit card is a special card that allows you to buy things without using cash. When you use a credit card to make a purchase, the credit company is lending you the money to pay for it. You can think of it as a small loan. Then, at the end of the month, you get a bill from the credit card company, and you have to pay back the borrowed money. If you don't pay the full amount, the credit card company will charge you interest on the remaining balance. Let's say you want to buy a laptop that costs $1,000, but you only have $200 saved up. You could use a credit card to make the purchase. The credit card company would lend you the remaining $800, and you could immediately take the laptop home. Then, when the credit card bill comes, you would need to pay back the $800 plus any interest that may be added.

Another form of credit is a loan. A loan is when you borrow a specific amount of money from a bank or another lender. When you take out a loan, you agree to repay the money over time, usually with monthly payments. Loans often have an interest rate, which is a percentage of the loan amount you have to pay in addition to the borrowed money. If you borrow more than you can afford to pay back, it can lead to debt and financial difficulties, so it's safer to only borrow what you really need and have a plan to pay it back on time.

Teens and Credit Cards

Teens can use credit cards, but usually, you need to be 18 years old to have your own credit card. That's because having a credit card involves legal stuff and being responsible with money, but there are still ways for you to learn about credit cards and start building your credit score before turning 18. One way is to become an authorized user on your parent's or guardian's credit card. It means you get a card linked to their account and can use it to make purchases. Your parent or guardian is responsible for paying the bills, but you can learn how to use credit wisely.

You can also investigate secured credit cards designed specifically for teens or students. These cards usually have lower spending limits and specific rules, but they can be a good way to start building a good credit score. Other ways you can build credit before turning 18 are:

1. **Open a Bank Account:** Start by opening a bank account in your name. This shows that you are ready to handle money.

2. **Get a Part-Time Job:** You get to earn your own money with a part-time job. It's a great way to show lenders that you have a source of income to repay any money you borrow.

3. **Pay Bills on Time:** Paying your bills, like your phone bill or streaming subscriptions, on time is another way. Late payments can hurt your credit score.

4. **Start Small:** Consider applying for a small loan, like a student or a small personal loan, if you need it for education or other essential purposes. Make sure to borrow

only what you need and pay it back on time.

5. **Monitor Your Credit:** Keep an eye on your credit report to make sure there are no errors or fraudulent activities. You can get a free copy of your credit report annually from any major credit bureau.

Responsible Credit Card Usage

Using a credit card can be exciting, but it must be used responsibly. Here are some helpful tips just for you on how to manage your credit card wisely, make payments on time, and avoid drowning in debt:

- **Create a Spending Plan:** Make a monthly budget that includes your income and expenses. This will help you understand your available money and how much you can comfortably spend using your credit card.

- **Set a Smart Credit Limit:** Decide on a sensible credit limit based on your income and what you can afford. Keeping your balance below 30% of your credit limit is generally a good idea. So, if your credit limit is $500, aim to keep your total balance below $150.

- **Make Timely Payments:** Very few things are more important than paying your monthly credit card bill on time and never missing a payment. Set reminders on your phone or use apps to notify you when your payment is due. Paying your bill in full each month is even better because it helps you avoid extra charges and build good credit.

- **Keep Track of Your Spending:** Stay on top of your credit card transactions by regularly checking your statements. Most credit card companies have user-friendly apps or online platforms that make it easy to monitor your transactions.

- **Avoid Paying Only the Minimum:** Whenever you can, try to pay more than the minimum amount due. If you only pay the minimum, it takes longer to pay off your balance, and you end up paying more interest charges. Paying more than the minimum helps you clear your debt faster.

- **Mind the Interest Rates:** Take note of the interest rates associated with your credit card. If you carry a balance from month to month, you'll be charged interest on that amount. To avoid paying interest, pay your entire balance before the due date.

- **Use Credit for What's Important:** Using your credit card for every little thing is tempting, but try to use it mainly for essential purchases. Save it for things like school supplies or emergencies rather than everyday small purchases. This way, you can manage your credit wisely and avoid unnecessary debt.

All You Need to Know about Credit Scores

Look at your credit score as a grade, showing how responsible you are with credit and how likely you are to repay borrowed money. This grade matters because it affects your ability to get loans, credit cards, and even rent an apartment. The key points below will help you understand credit scores and maintain a good one.

1. **Paying on Time:** Pay your bills, including credit card payments and any other debts, on time. Late or missed payments can bring your credit score down. Staying organized and making timely payments is a great way to build a positive credit history.

2. **Length of Credit History:** The length of time you've had credit accounts also matters. Lenders like to see a longer credit history because it shows you have experience managing credit responsibly. If you're just starting out, don't worry. Focus on building a positive credit history over time. The longer you have credit, the better it

looks on your score.

3. **Variety of Credit:** Having different types of credit, like credit cards and loans, can be good for your credit score. It shows that you can handle different financial responsibilities. Regardless, only take on credit that you genuinely need and can manage responsibly. Don't go overboard by opening too many accounts.

4. **Check Your Credit Reports:** Monitoring your credit reports regularly is a good habit. Reviewing your reports helps you spot any errors or mistakes that could hurt your score. If you find any, you can take steps to correct them.

5. **Be Cautious with Applications:** When you apply for new credit, like a credit card or a loan, it results in what's called a hard inquiry on your credit report. Too many hard inquiries in a short time can lower your credit score. Apply for credit only when you really need it, and avoid too many applications all at once.

6. **Build Healthy Financial Habits:** At the end of the day, maintaining a good credit score is about practicing responsible financial habits. Create a budget, save money, and be mindful of your spending. By being wise with your money, you'll be better equipped to handle credit responsibly and maintain a strong credit score.

What Debt Is and How to Deal with It

Debt is when you borrow money and have to pay it back later, usually with interest. You have that financial responsibility because you had an agreement. Now, debt can be a bit tricky, which is why it must be handled with care. Here's why managing and reducing debt effectively is a big deal:

1. **Interest Payments:** When you borrow money, the lender adds interest to the amount you owe. And guess what? That interest can really add up over time. If you only make minimum payments or let your balance grow, you could pay way more than

you initially borrowed, and that's not a fun situation.

2. **Financial Stress:** Having a lot of debt can be stressful. When a big chunk of your hard-earned money goes towards debt payments, it can limit your ability to cover other expenses, save, or treat yourself. You deserve to enjoy your life without the stress of debt. Managing debt properly can reduce that stress and give you more financial freedom.

3. **Credit Score Impact:** Your credit score is a report card for lenders, and it's affected by your debt management habits. If you have high debt and miss payments, it can bring down your credit score, making it harder to get approved for loans or credit cards in the future. If you do get approved, you could be charged higher interest rates.

4. **Missed Opportunities:** Debt can put a damper on your dreams. It can make it harder to realize big goals like buying your own place or starting a business. It can even affect your ability to save for the future.

Techniques for a Debt Repayment Plan

Creating a personalized debt repayment plan is a step toward reducing unnecessary debt. Here are some strategies and techniques to help you develop a plan that suits your financial situation:

- **Know Your Debts:** Take stock of any money you owe. Make a list of your debts, including the amounts, interest rates, and due dates. This will give you a clear picture of what you need to tackle.

- **Set Goals:** Think about what you want to achieve financially. Maybe you want to buy a car or make an investment. Having goals will keep you motivated to pay off your debts and make wise financial choices.

- **Create a Budget:** Start by tracking your income and expenses. Figure out how much money is coming in and where it's going. This will help you understand how much you can allocate towards monthly debt repayment. Look for areas where you can cut back on expenses to free up more money for debt payments.

- **Prioritize Your Debts:** Decide which debts to tackle first. You can choose to pay off the ones with the smallest balances or the ones with the highest interest rates. Focusing on one debt at a time will make you progress faster and feel more motivated to keep going.

- **Talk to Your Creditors:** If you're having trouble making payments, don't be afraid to reach out to your creditors. Explain your situation and see if they can help. They may be willing to work with you to find a solution. They can consider adjusting your payment plan or reducing interest rates.

- **Find Ways to Earn Money:** Get a part-time job or do odd jobs to increase your income. This extra money can be put towards your debts and help you pay them off faster.

- **Avoid Unnecessary Debt:** Always be cautious about taking on new debt. Avoid impulse purchases and think really hard before paying for anything non-essential. It's easy to get caught up in wanting new things just because you have a credit card, but remember that it is easier to borrow than to pay back.

Credit Card Alternatives

If you're looking for ways to avoid debt and repayment issues without using credit cards, here are some cool alternatives to consider:

- **Debit Cards:** Think of debit cards as electronic versions of your piggy bank. With a debit card, you spend money directly from your bank account. You'll be using your own cash, so you won't end up owing anyone later. Just make sure you have enough money in your account before you swipe.

- **Cash:** This one is straightforward. By using cash for your purchases, you can only spend the money you have. There is no need to worry about repayments or debt. Just count your cash, hand it over, and you're good to go.

- **Prepaid Cards:** Prepaid cards are gift cards but for yourself. You load them up with a specific amount of money, and then you can use them to pay for things. The cool part is that you can't spend more than what's on the card. You have a spending limit that keeps you from going overboard.

- **Automatic Savings Accounts:** You can set up an automatic savings account where a portion of your income is transferred monthly. By saving up, you won't have to rely on credit cards and get stuck with debt.

Chapter Six: Overcoming Financial Challenges

You've just received your allowance or paycheck, and you're super stoked to spend it on that awesome thing you've been thinking about. But wait, before you do that, you should know about all the things that can get in the way of that. These things are called financial obstacles. Here are a few of them to pay attention to:

- **Debt:** First, there's debt. Borrowing money from friends and parents a little too often can lead to too much debt, leaving you with less money than you hoped to spend.

- **Low Income:** Have you ever had that moment when you want to buy something you really want, but your wallet feels like it's on a diet? That's what it's like when you don't have enough income to cover your expenses. You basically have a leaky bucket that keeps draining your money faster than it comes in. So, finding ways to increase your income, like getting a part-time job or starting a small business, can help you fill that bucket.

- **Emergencies:** Life is full of surprises, and sometimes these surprises come with a price tag. These unexpected expenses can feel like hitting a roadblock when you least expect it. That's why having an emergency fund is always a good idea.

- **Ignorance:** Knowledge is power. You can't solve a puzzle without knowing what the pieces mean. You need more knowledge and more financial education. Learning about personal finance topics like investing, taxes, and credit can help you understand the puzzle pieces and make better financial decisions.

- **Consumerism:** Finally, peer pressure and consumerism. That feeling when you want to fit in with your friends and buy whatever is in vogue? That's being pulled into a spending frenzy. But if you can remember to prioritize your needs over your wants and make conscious spending choices, the pressure won't sway you as hard.

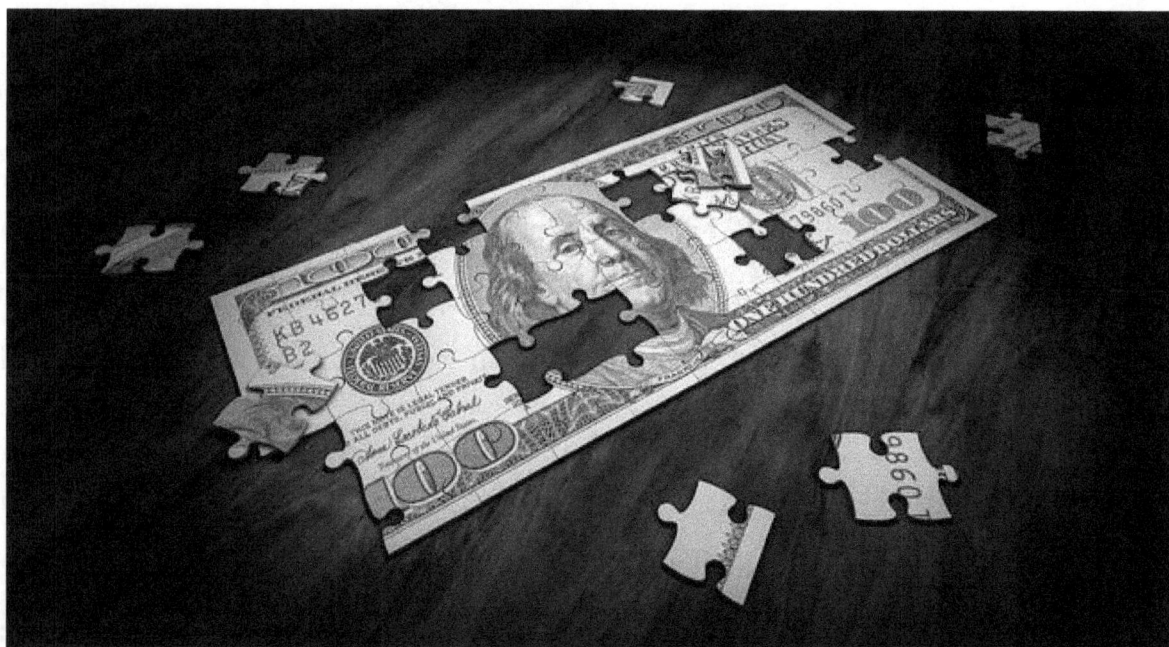

Make sure to always get rid of your financial obstacles before spending and enjoying your money.
https://pixabay.com/photos/puzzle-money-business-finance-2500328/

Financial Challenges and Your Health

Financial problems can mess with your emotions and general health. Constantly feeling stressed, anxious, or on edge because of money will negatively affect your happiness and peace of mind. Your relationships are also at stake. Financial issues tend to cause fights and tension with family, friends, or even your crush, making it hard to enjoy time with the people you care about. Fixing your money problems can help make your relationships healthier and happier.

Financial obstacles also limit your opportunities and stop you from growing. If you're always struggling to make ends meet, it's tough to go after your dreams, learn new things, or invest in yourself. It's like being stuck in a small box, unable to spread your wings and reach your full potential. If you ignore these obstacles instead of facing them head-on, you limit yourself even further.

Do you need more reasons to deal with money problems directly instead of ignoring them? Face your problems, and you will be:

1. **Building Toughness:** Facing financial challenges head-on helps you become stronger and better at handling tough situations. The more you take charge early on, the better you get at bouncing back from difficult situations.

2. **Securing Your Future:** Solving money problems as a teen sets you up for a better future. It helps you learn how to manage your money better – making a budget, saving up, and making smart money moves. If you can take control of your finances now, you are increasing your chances for a brighter and more secure future for yourself.

3. **Reducing Stress:** When you proactively sort out your money problems, you feel less stressed and anxious. When you are in control of your money, you automatically feel

calm and confident. A weight is lifted off your shoulders, and you feel more at ease.

4. **Strengthening Relationships:** Open and honest conversations about money build trust and better communication with your family and friends. It also lets you ask for help and support when needed, making your relationships stronger.

Tips for Spotting Any Financial Problems

- **Track Your Spending:** Keep a record of your expenses for a few weeks or a month. Write down everything you spend money on, no matter how small. This will help you see where your money is going and identify any areas where you may be overspending.

- **Assess Your Income and Expenses:** Look at how much money you earn or receive as allowances. Then, compare it to your expenses. Are you spending more than you're earning? Are there any unnecessary expenses that you can cut back on? Understanding your income and expenses will give you a clear picture of your financial situation.

- **Recognize Patterns and Habits:** Look for patterns in your spending behavior. Do you tend to overspend on clothes, eating out, or entertainment? Are there any impulsive buying habits you need to be aware of? Checking these patterns will help you understand your spending habits better.

- **Review Your Financial Goals:** Think about your short-term and long-term financial goals. Do you want to save up for something specific, like a new phone or a laptop? Are you planning for college or other future expenses? Understanding your goals will help you prioritize your spending and make better financial decisions.

- **Ask for Advice from Adults You Trust:** Talk to your parents, guardians, or other trusted adults about your financial situation. They serve as pillars of guidance and support and can give valuable advice based on their experiences. If you need help, don't hesitate to ask for it.

- **Educate Yourself:** Find time to learn about personal finance topics. Read books and articles, or watch videos that teach you more about budgeting, saving, investing, and other money management skills. The more you educate yourself, the easier this will be for you.

- **Use Digital Tools and Apps:** Different digital options exist, such as budgeting apps or expense trackers. These apps are designed to make managing your money simple and even fun. They'll help you see where your money is going. That way, you can better decide how to save and spend. You'll find apps that remind you when your bills are due, show you how much you've spent on coffee or video games, and help you set savings goals for that summer trip or monthly subscription.

- **Take Advantage of Financial Literacy Resources:** There are workshops, seminars, and courses on financial literacy specifically designed for teenagers. Many organizations and financial institutions offer resources and programs to help young people improve their money management skills. The first step to overcoming financial problems is to be aware. When you notice and understand your financial challenges, dealing with them becomes easier than you think.

Common Financial Obstacles and Solutions

Everyone faces financial obstacles at some point, but having a plan can make a big difference. By saving, budgeting, and doing better with your money, you'll be well on your way to dodging these obstacles. Take it one step at a time and give these solutions a shot:

Job Hunting

1. **Know Your Worth:** When looking for a job, research and understand the average salaries for the jobs you're interested in. This knowledge will help you negotiate fair compensation.

2. **Develop Negotiation Skills:** Practice negotiating your worth with friends or family. As always, confidence is key.

3. **Be Open to Mentorship:** Connect with successful women in fields you're interested in. They can guide you through pay negotiations and career advancement.

Building Savings

1. **Set Financial Goals:** Determine what you're saving for, whether it's an emergency fund, college expenses, or prom.

2. **Create a Budget:** Track your income and expenses to see where your money goes. Identify areas where you can spend less to save more.

3. **Automate Savings:** Set up automatic transfers from your checking account to a savings account. This way, you'll consistently save without thinking about it.

Managing Student Loans

1. **Understand Loan Terms:** Get familiar with the details of your student loans, such as interest rates, repayment plans, and any available forgiveness options.

2. **Make a Payment Plan:** Create a budget that includes monthly loan payments. Try paying more than the minimum whenever possible to reduce interest costs.

3. **Explore Loan Repayment Assistance:** Look into programs that can help lower your loan payments, such as income-driven repayment plans or loan forgiveness programs.

Investing for the Future

1. **Educate Yourself:** Learn more about the basics of investing, such as stocks, bonds, and mutual funds. Books and podcasts are great starting points.

2. **Start Small:** Begin investing with a small amount of money you're comfortable using.

3. **Maintain a Long-Term Perspective:** Stay focused on your long-term goals and resist making impulsive decisions based on short-term market fluctuations.

Developing Financial Confidence

1. **Find Ways to Know More:** Take advantage of financial literacy resources, podcasts, and books that empower you with knowledge about money management.

2. **Practice Budgeting:** Track your spending, set financial goals, and regularly review your budget to reaffirm your confidence in managing your money.

3. **Surround Yourself with Supportive Networks:** Associate with other girls and women focused on financial empowerment. Listen to their experiences, tips, and encouragement. There's no shame in asking for help. Reach out and take advantage of the available help. You deserve support and the opportunity to do better.

Chapter Seven: Making Money as a Teen

Every teenager is standing at the crossroads of independence and responsibility. You yearn for a taste of freedom while simultaneously grappling with the need to fund an ever-growing list of desires. Fortunately for you, gone are the days of relying solely on allowances and inconsistent odd jobs for a few bucks here and there. It's about time you unshackle your inner entrepreneur and take control of your financial destiny.

It's about time you unshackle your inner entrepreneur and take control of your financial destiny.
https://www.pexels.com/photo/person-holding-fan-of-us-dollar-bills-4968655/

You can start making money doing something you love. Maybe it's turning your knack for baking into a flourishing cupcake business, leveraging your tech skills to offer website design services, or even monetizing your passion for fashion through YouTube; the options are limitless. This chapter is focused on thinking outside the box, capitalizing on your unique talents, and discovering creative ways to turn your gifts and strengths into cold, hard cash.

But hold on . . . do you even know why you should even bother making money as a teen? Aside from the obvious perks of financial independence and the ability to afford those luxuries, the mission of entrepreneurial experimentation also presents invaluable life lessons. Through trial and error, you'll learn the art of budgeting, time management, marketing, customer service, and much more. Plus, the satisfaction of building something from scratch and seeing it blossom is an unparalleled feeling of accomplishment. So, prepare yourself to seize the opportunities and take the first steps on a path where you are the architect of your financial success.

Legal Ways to Make Money in Your Area

If you want to make money in your neighborhood, there are plenty of safe and legal ways. You can try:

1. **Babysitting:** Many parents need someone mature and responsible to watch their kids. They have errands to run, date nights to attend, or simply need a break from the constant commotion of parenting. That's where you come in. You'll spend your evenings or weekends playing games, reading stories, and having fun with energetic and imaginative children. You get to be their role model, playmate, and trusted guardian. Parents want to feel confident that their babies are in good hands. So, be sure to demonstrate your responsibility by learning some basic first-aid techniques and having emergency contact numbers handy. This way, parents will have peace of mind, and you'll feel more optimistic about handling any unexpected situations.

2. **Lawn Care and Gardening:** Many neighbors and busy homeowners are looking for reliable help with their lawns, gardens, and outdoor spaces. They need someone who can mow their lawns, pull weeds, trim hedges, or lend a hand with other gardening duties. Knock on doors, put up flyers, or ask your parents if you can post about your services on community bulletin boards or social media groups. The demand for a reliable and enthusiastic lawn care guru is higher than you think.

3. **Pet Sitting and Dog Walking:** Too many pet owners have busy lives or travel plans that keep them away from their beloved companions. They need someone trustworthy and caring to step in and take care of their furry friends. Your job

description will include walking dogs, playing fetch, and providing companionship to pets while their owners are away.

4. **Tutoring:** If you're good at a specific subject or skill, why not help other students who could use extra support? You can offer one-on-one or group tutoring sessions. The best part is that tutoring is flexible. You can set your own schedule and choose how many students you want to work with. It can be a side gig while you're still in school, or you can dedicate more time to it during breaks or weekends.

5. **House Cleaning and Organizing:** Busy people often juggle a million things at once, and sometimes, cleaning or organizing their homes falls to the bottom of their to-do list. You can offer your services to help with tasks like dusting, vacuuming, or decluttering. Not only will you earn money, but you'll also become a pro at time management, attention to detail, and problem-solving. Plus, you'll learn how to work independently and take pride in a job well done.

Making Money Online

If you're curious about expanding your network and making money online, you're in for a treat. You might have heard of YouTubers who started their channels as teens and have turned their enthusiasm into a successful online business. They create videos about topics they love, like gaming, fashion, beauty, or educational content. As their channel grows, they earn money through ads, sponsorships, and merchandise sales. One fantastic example is a YouTuber named Carmen. She started making videos about her favorite things and sharing tips and tricks. Her channel gained a lot of subscribers, and now, at a young age, she makes a living doing what she loves and entertaining her audience.

Success on YouTube or in any other online space takes time and effort. It's about more than just making money. These successful entrepreneurs are creating content that connects with people and building a tribe around their interests. So, if you have abilities that you want to share with the world, don't be afraid to give it a shot and start creating your own online presence.

That said, here are a few other ways for you to make money online:

1. **Get Crafty and Sell Your Creations:** If you love making DIYs such as jewelry, accessories, or artwork, you can set up an online store on platforms like Etsy. It's your own little shop where people can buy your handiwork.

2. **Share Your Writing Skills:** If you enjoy writing, you can become a freelance writer or start a blog. You can write articles or blog posts for websites or share your thoughts and experiences on your own blog. It's a great way to express yourself and make money while you're at it.

3. **Show Off Your Social Media Skills:** If you love being in front of the camera or have a flair for creating engaging content on platforms like Instagram or TikTok, you can become a social media influencer. Brands might want to work with you to promote their products or services. So, you get paid to be yourself and share amazing content with your followers.

4. **Tutor or Teach Online:** If you're good at a subject or have the skill to share, you can offer online tutoring or teaching services. You can help younger students with homework or teach them something you know extremely well, like playing an instrument or speaking a foreign language.

5. **Help with Virtual Tasks:** Many entrepreneurs and small businesses need help with administrative tasks like organizing data or managing social media. You can offer your services as a virtual assistant and help them out. It's a way to earn money while being organized and tech-savvy.

Advice and Hacks for Making Money Online

- **Be Your Amazing, Authentic Self:** You don't have to pretend to be someone you're not. Just be yourself. Embrace your quirks and let them shine in everything you do. People love genuine content, so stay true to who you are.

- **Find Your Passion and Niche:** Discover what you love and what excites you. Whether it's history, music, art, or something else, focus on what makes you happy. When you create content about things you genuinely enjoy, it attracts others who share the same interests.

- **Stay Consistent:** Building a following and making money online takes patience and dedication. Stay consistent with your content creation and engagement. Post regularly, interact with your audience, and be dependable. Consistency shows your effort and helps you grow a loyal community.

- **Save and Budget Like a Professional:** Financial advisors will always advise you to save and budget wisely. When you start earning money online, set aside some for savings and manage your expenses carefully. Create a budget that lets you enjoy your earnings while planning for the future.

- **Invest in Yourself:** Don't be afraid to invest in your skills and personal growth. Take courses, join webinars, or read books that help you improve your content creation, marketing, or financial know-how. Learning new things can give you an edge and open up exciting prospects.

- **Collaborate and Connect:** Connecting with other creators, influencers, and professionals is valuable. Collaborating with others can introduce you to new audiences and teach you from their experiences. Networking can lead to incredible collaborations or mentorship opportunities. So, don't wait to reach out, support others, and develop authentic relationships.

- **Take Care of You:** Making money online is cool, but don't forget about your mental and physical health. Take breaks when you need them, practice self-care, and find a balance between your online presence and other activities. Your happiness and health matter more than all the likes in the world.

- **Be Open to Making Mistakes and Learning from Them:** Don't let disappointments get you down. Mistakes happen to everyone, even successful people making tons of money online. Learn from your slip-ups, bounce back, and keep moving forward. Each mistake is a chance to grow and become even better.

- **Keep It Real with Your Audience:** Building a loyal community is all about connecting with your audience. Respond to their comments, ask for their opinions, and make them feel special. Engage in conversations and create a supportive space. Your followers are the ones who will cheer you on as you reach for the stars.

Chapter Eight: Long-Term Financial Goals

Close your eyes for a minute and imagine the life you want – the adventures you'll have, the places you'll go, and the impact you'll make. If you can envision your future, you'll have a clear direction to focus on. Whatever vision you have for yourself, you can make it as big as your mind can imagine because anything is possible. There is so much waiting for you in the future. Have you ever thought about what retirement might look like for you? Have you pictured yourself enjoying your golden years, traveling, chilling, and living comfortably? Or maybe you've dreamed of owning your own home – a place to express yourself and create lasting memories. Do you want to go to school and get degree after degree after degree? And for those entrepreneurial spirits, do you see yourself running a business, taking risks, and reaping the rewards? Maybe you see yourself surrounded by a loving family, cherishing every moment and creating a legacy that will be remembered for generations. Whatever your dreams may be, recognize that they are within your reach if you play your cards right.

Whatever your dreams may be, recognize that they are within your reach if you play your cards right.

https://pixabay.com/photos/business-plan-monitor-wall-3219705/

You might be thinking, "I'm just a teenager. Why should I start planning now?" Early planning is the secret behind all the self-made millionaires and billionaires you've heard about. By starting now, you'll have more time to save, invest, and make brilliant financial decisions. Plus, breaking down your big goals into smaller steps makes them less overwhelming and more achievable. This will be the blueprint for your future, and you can design it as glamorous and detailed as you want.

Types of Long-Term Goals

There is no limit to the long-term goals you can set for yourself. Here are a few to think about:

- **Retirement:** There will come a time when you can kick back and enjoy life without worrying about work. Preparing for your retirement should involve planning so you can have financial freedom and do the things you love. You might be traveling, learning a new hobby, or spending time with your loved ones. Saving for retirement now means you'll have a comfortable future waiting for you.

- **Homeownership:** Have you ever dreamed of having a place that's truly yours? Owning a home gives you a sense of stability and the freedom to decorate and make it your own. Plus, as you pay off your home, you're building up an investment in yourself.

- **Education:** Going to college, trade school, or getting advanced degrees will give you the knowledge and skills for a successful career. It's an investment in yourself and can boost your future earning potential.

- **Starting a Business:** Are you a budding entrepreneur? Starting your own business is both daunting and thrilling. It lets you turn your strengths into a career and be your own boss. You can create something incredible and maybe even achieve financial independence with hard work and determination.

Creating a Financial Plan

It's time to talk about creating a financial plan, and it's much easier than you might think. Here are some broken-down and easy steps you can follow:

- **Set Clear Goals:** Start by deciding what you want to achieve with your money. Whatever it is, be specific about it so you have an idea of where you're headed.

- **Make a Budget:** The value of a budget can't be overstated when creating a financial plan for your future. Don't forget to allocate money for savings, too. The goal is to spend less than you earn so you can save and reach your goals faster.

- **Save, Save, Save:** The money you save up will come through for you when you least expect it, so always have a savings account. Even small amounts add up over time.

- **Be a Smart Shopper:** When you're shopping, be mindful of your spending. Compare prices, look for discounts, and ask yourself if you really need something before buying it. Treating yourself occasionally is fun, but being mindful of your spending habits will help you stay on track with your financial goals.

- **Learn about Investing:** As you get older, you can start learning about different investment options. If you know more, you can do more.

- **Stay Informed:** Keep learning about personal finance. Read books, follow finance pages or podcasts, and ask questions.

Strategies for Overcoming Obstacles and Setbacks

Of course, there could be a few hurdles that pop up when trying to reach your financial goals, but knowing what you could face can help you find your way through each and every one of them. You might experience:

1. **Limited Income:** As a teenager, your income might be limited to allowances or part-time jobs. It can feel challenging to save or invest when you're not raking in big bucks.

2. **Peer Pressure:** Friends and social media can sometimes make people feel they need to spend money on things they don't need. It's easy to get caught up in the latest trends or try to keep up with everyone else.

3. **Impulse Spending:** Those impulse buys can sneak up on you. One minute, you're browsing online, and the next, you've clicked "buy now" on something you hadn't planned for.

Thankfully, there are practical strategies and handy hacks to help you overcome these temptations and stay on track with your plan.

- **Prioritize Needs Over Wants:** You know you don't need those shoes; you just want them. Distinguish between what you truly need and what you simply want. Focus on fulfilling your needs before indulging in your wants.

- **Delay Gratification:** Practice patience and avoid impulsive purchases. Wait a day or two before buying something to determine if it's a genuine necessity or just a passing impulse.

- **Avoid Tempting Environments:** Stay away from places or situations that encourage unnecessary spending. Opt for activities that don't revolve around spending money.

- **Identify Triggers:** Recognize the situations or emotions that lead you to make impulsive financial decisions. Once you identify them, find healthier alternatives to cope with those triggers.

- **Use Cash Instead of Cards:** Use cash as much as you can for your day-to-day expenses. Physical money makes spending feel more tangible and can help you stick to your budget.

- **Practice Contentment:** Focus on gratitude for what you have rather than constantly craving more.

- **Limit Your Exposure to Advertising:** Be mindful of the advertisements you're exposed to. Limit the time you spend browsing shopping platforms or watching commercials that might tempt you to spend unnecessarily.

- **Avoid Comparison Traps:** Resist the urge to compare your financial situation or possessions with others. Focus on your progress and what brings you true happiness.

- **Believe in Yourself:** You've got what it takes to overcome any challenge. Believe in your abilities and know that setbacks are just temporary bumps on the way to success.

- **Learn from Your Mistakes:** When things don't go as planned, take a moment to reflect. There will always be something to learn from any situation, and that knowledge will be invaluable to making better choices in the future.

Conclusion

As you reach the end of this transformative journey, remember that personal finance is not a one-time thing. It is life-long, and it is forever. You now have a solid foundation to build upon, and you should feel empowered and excited to make your own choices about your money, especially as you get older. Thank you for choosing this book and staying committed to your financial education. No one is more in charge of your future and finances than you are, and as you've explored the world of personal finance and money management, you've uncovered the secrets to getting off to a solid start. You've learned about budgeting, saving, investing, and planning for the future you deserve. But more importantly, you've discovered the power within every fiber of your being – a power that can help you control your financial destiny.

As you say goodbye to these pages, know that success is not defined by the numbers in your bank account or the things you own. True success comes from the delicate balance between your financial decisions, values, and dreams. It is the freedom to follow your passions and support yourself fearlessly. Keep expanding your financial knowledge. Don't stop looking for opportunities to grow. You can read more books, attend workshops, or connect with mentors who can guide you on this journey. Surround yourself with friends who uplift and inspire you, and always remember that mistakes are part of the learning process.

Believe in yourself because your commitment to knowledge at this young age sets you apart, and there's no doubt that you are capable of greater things than you can possibly imagine right now. You hold the power to shape your financial future, and with determination and perseverance, you can crush anything that tries to stop you.

Check out another book in the series

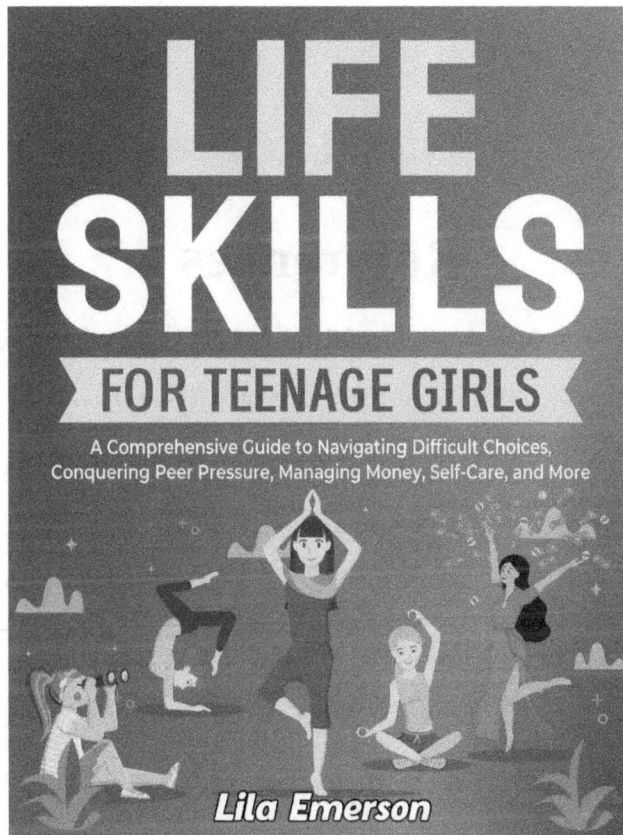

LIFE SKILLS

FOR TEENAGE GIRLS

A Comprehensive Guide to Navigating Difficult Choices, Conquering Peer Pressure, Managing Money, Self-Care, and More

Lila Emerson

References

CPA, E. H., CFA, CFP®. (2018, March 29). *10 Money Management Tips for Teens.* Echo Wealth Management. https://www.echowealthmanagement.com/blog/10-money-management-tips-teens

Oh, H. (2022, August 11). *These are the best ways for teenagers to save money with (or without) a job.* Seventeen. https://www.seventeen.com/life/school/a40670024/how-to-save-money-teenager/

Peacock, C. (2023, April 3). *10 Essential Credit Tips for Teens to Know.* Gohenry. https://www.gohenry.com/uk/blog/financial-education/credit-tips-teens

Rosenthal, Jack.(2019, December 13) *Teen Investing.*

Shanku Mahato. (2021, July 2) *1000 Ways to Make Money Online.*